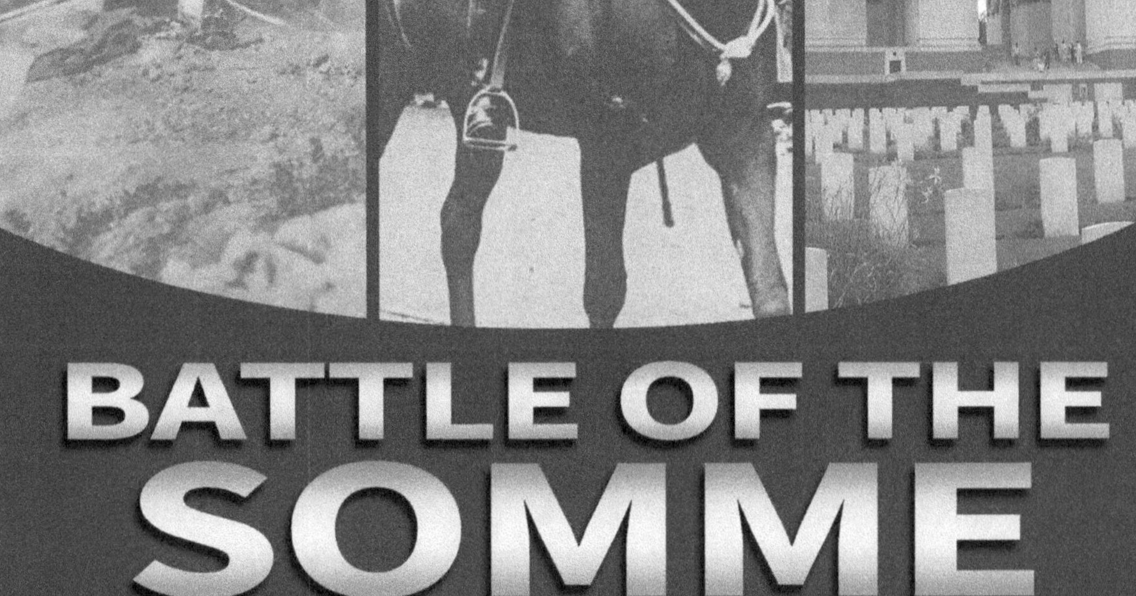

BATTLE OF THE SOMME

A BRIEF HISTORY FROM BEGINNING TO END

HISTORY HUB

Bonus Downloads

Get Free Books with **<u>Any Purchase</u>** *History Shorts*

Every purchase comes with a FREE download!

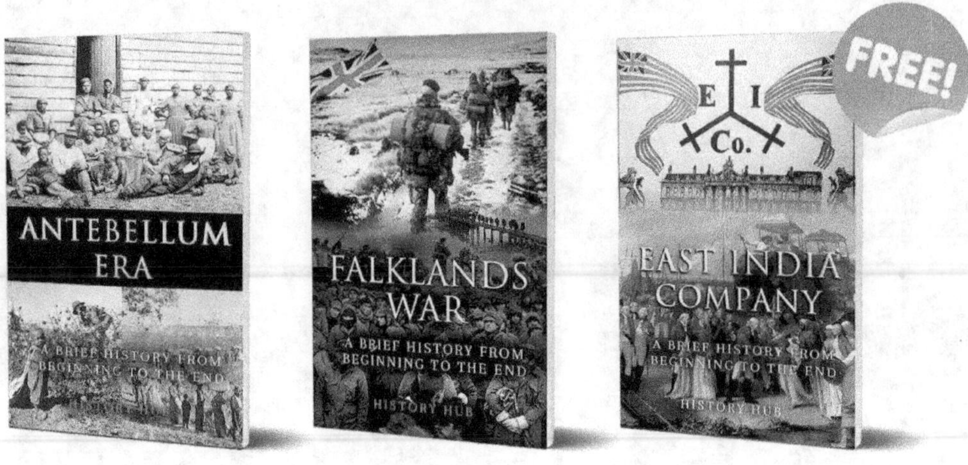

Battle of the Somme

A Brief History from Beginning to the End

History Shorts

CONTENTS

Chapter One

Introduction

The Battle of the Somme 1 July 1916 to 18 November 1916

Anthem for Doomed Youth

by Wilfred Owen

What passing bells for these who die as cattle?

— Only the monstrous anger of the guns.

Only the stuttering rifles' rapid rattle

Can patter out their hasty orisons.

No mockeries now for them; no prayers nor bells;

Nor any voice of mourning save the choirs, —

The shrill, demented choirs of wailing shells;

And bugles calling for them from sad shires.

What candles may be held to speed them all?

Not in the hands of boys, but in their eyes

Shall shine the holy glimmers of goodbyes.

The pallor of girls' brows shall be their pall;

Their flowers the tenderness of patient minds,

And each slow dusk a drawing-down of blinds.

The First World War, particularly the Battle of the Somme, was a time of terrible tragedy and loss of life. Whether it needlessly shed blood or whether the losses were justified by the first Allied victory is something we'll be exploring in this history of the Battle of Somme.

The Battle of the Somme was originally meant to be an easy victory by the British and French armies against the German forces on the Western Front. At the end of 1915, relentless German pressure on the French in the Verdun region meant that the Allies had to look for a way to try and deflect the German attack. Because the French were already besieged on the Verdun front, it meant that Britain had to deflect some of the pressure through the Battle of the Somme, which took place on the upper part of the Somme River. They inflicted heavy bombardment on the Germans for days before the attack and expected an easy breakthrough and retreat of the German forces. Instead, they became deadlocked in a bloody battle that lasted for 141 days. During that period, more than a million men from both sides were either killed, wounded, or captured. On the first day of the battle alone, British deaths stood at 19 240 and the number of wounded brought the number up to more than 57 000. It was without a doubt the bloodiest day ever in the history of the British Army. The Somme, much like Verdun for the French, still plays an important part in the minds of the British people, and for many people, it represents the futility of war and the waste of human life.

History has differing opinions on this though. While many people believe it to be true that it was a futile and pointless battle, war historians believe that the lessons taught at the Somme would ultimately secure the Allied victory. It's not definitive who actually won the battle but it's quite clear who won the war. Whether it was worth it or not will depend on your personal take on the importance of even fighting the First World War and, in fact, which side you were on.

The casualties of war were not only physical, however. It's only in later history that the long-term mental effects of having witnessed the horrors of battles like the Somme have come under the spotlight. Many psychologists believe that a whole generation of emotionally dysfunctional men arose because of witnessing and being part of such horrors.

Mental Cases

by Wilfred Owen

—These are men whose minds the Dead have ravished.

Memory fingers in their hair of murders,

Multitudinous murders they once witnessed.

Wading sloughs of flesh these helpless wander,

Treading blood from lungs that had loved laughter.

Always they must see these things and hear them,

Batter of guns and shatter of flying muscles,

Carnage incomparable and human squander

Rucked too thick for these men's extrication.

This excerpt from a poem by Wilfred Owen, while not his most famous, looks not only at the terrible carnage of war but also at the effects that linger in the minds of those who have not lost their lives but are haunted ever after by the horrors that have been witnessed. War takes casualties in every way. Wilfred Owen himself was killed in action in France in 1918.

We'll be taking a close look, not only at the battle itself but at whether it was a strategic victory or not, and finally, based on the horrifying effects of war, whether it can ever be justified.

Chapter Two
The Battle of the Somme - Horrifying Statistics and Strange Facts

The Battle of the Somme will go down in history as the bloodiest, most horrifying battle in the history of Britain. While the British genuinely did not anticipate the extent of German resistance, since they had already subjected them to a week of artillery attack, they proved to be gravely mistaken.

The initial attack on 1 July 1916 was launched by 120 000 Allied troops from England and its colonies like South Africa, Australia, India, New Zealand, Canada, and Newfoundland. Of those 120 000 soldiers, 20 000 were killed on the first day. Most of them were killed in the first hour, and 37 000 soldiers were wounded. A man was killed every 4.4 seconds. The tally at the end of the day showed that 37 pairs of British brothers were killed on that first day. One can just imagine the heartbreak for the families at home. This was the single bloodiest day in the history of British battles.

The Battle of the Somme lasted 141 days and has been classified as a War of Attrition, where forces on both sides tried to wear one another down by a relentless loss of lives, men in action, and equipment. The mental and physical drain on the soldiers was terrible as the war dragged from summer into fall, and the rains created an absolute mire that the men could not escape. "We live in a world of Somme mud. We sleep in it, work in it, fight in it, wade in it and many of us die in it. We see it, feel it, eat it and curse it, but we can't escape it, not even by dying," Australian soldier Edward Lynch once recounted.

Over that period, the Allied forces launched more than 90 attacks before the battle was called off on 18 November by Sir Douglas Haig, the commander-in-chief of the British forces. Over 141 days, the British forces only managed to advance six miles.

The overall casualties from both sides for this period were more than a million with more than 300 000 deaths. The British troops had 420 000 casualties, including the deaths of 125 000 men. The French casualties were 200 000, and the Germans lost 500 000 men to death or injury.

Interestingly, the Battle of the Somme was the first time the tanks were used during a war. Thirty-two Mark 1 tanks were deployed by the British in an attack in early September. Although they were armed with machine guns or cannons, they failed to break the deadlock. They were two slow and ungainly and often broke down. Improved designs made the tank a formidable weapon in World War Two, but its first designs were less than effective.

Another strange statistic about the Somme was the use of "Pals Battalions." The War office initially encouraged men to volunteer to serve by getting neighbors, families, and friends to enlist together. So many close communities were devastated by the losses at the Somme that this idea was disbanded. Of the *Accrington Pals*, 584 men of the 720 members were killed or wounded in half an hour, while the *Grimsby Chums* sustained more than 500 casualties on the first day of the battle.

General Henry Rawlinson, ordered the inexperienced troops to walk slowly in orderly, evenly spaced lines, carrying only their swagger sticks or revolvers. Experienced commanders ignored this directive, and many inexperienced troops marched to their deaths without having a chance to fight. This just shows the ignorance which manifested in the planning of the War directly impacted on the extremely heavy casualties.

One particularly strange story was one of the soccer balls. Captain Wilfred Nevill decided to encourage his soldiers from the 8th East Surreys by presenting each of the four platoons with a soccer ball and promising an award for the first platoon to kick it into the German trenches. The balls were bravely painted by the troops. There was the East Surreys v The Bavarians and *The Great European Cup* among others. At zero hour when the whistles were blown, the East Surreys kicked their balls bravely forward but the carnage was inevitable. Poor Captain Nevill was shot in the head and found lying next to two soccer balls. Seven other officers and countless troops died.

Even top government officials did not escape tragedy. The Prime Minister of England, Herbert Asquith lost his son Raymond from a bullet wound to the chest while leading his men over the line. Two other members of the British parliament were killed at Somme, and Harold Macmillan who would later become Britain's Prime Minister was wounded twice while he was part of the Grenadiers.

A young Adolf Hitler was wounded in the leg at the Somme. One can't help wondering what might have happened if he had met the fate of many of his fellows. The young Corporal Hilter called the Battle of the Somme "more like hell than war." He was sent to a German Hospital to convalesce although he didn't apparently want to go.

These stories show us a personal face to the Battle of Somme where young men, barely ready to leave school, tried to put on a brave face despite the terrible circumstances in which they found themselves.

Chapter Three
The History Behind World War I

If you ask most people what caused World War I, they will tell you that it was the assassination of the Archduke Franz by a Serbian militant, and you'd be right to wonder why that should have caused horrors like the Battle of the Somme, but like most things in life, events happen because of a long build-up of tensions and incidents that eventually result in a catalyst.

The factors that caused WWI included:

Nationalism. This is the root cause of WWI because it is the love and passion that people have for their own country and the rejection of a threat to it by other nations. It takes time, however, for countries to decide that their personal love for their country is sufficient to create a war over it.

Germany at this time was particularly militant and very proud of its new unified status after the Franco-Prussian war of 1812 and the unification of the German states into the German Empire in 1871. The Germans felt that they were an unstoppable world power, and France, after several humiliating defeats, had no stomach to allow them to continue. Russia, at this juncture, was protecting the growth of pan-slavism which entailed the unification of the Slavic people and made the area around Serbia very unstable. The Serbians wished to create an independent state which made the area around the Balkans a veritable ticking time bomb, called the "Balkan Powder Keg."

This also led to the more general spread of nationalism not only across Europe but even into Asia as more and more countries joined WWI to prove their own power and dominance. This changed the face of the war which became increasingly complex and prolonged.

Imperialism was the next long-term cause of WWI. Imperialism is the domination of one country over the ideas, culture, economy, and politics of another country.

WWI happened at a time of heavy competition for colonies by European countries, especially England. Germany was trying to control parts of Africa in areas that were already circled by colonies of England and France.

When Germany tried to stop France from establishing a protectorate over Morocco in 1911, Britain and France became closer allies in an attempt to stop German imperialism and grow their own.

Militarism. The growth of nationalism and imperialism led to increasing militarism. An arms race began with the development of a whole new style of highly armed warships and the training of bigger armies.

By 1914, Germany had more than 2 million soldiers and 100 warships. Great Britain increased her navies. An attitude of militarism, particularly in Russia and Germany also affected the attitude of the population, making them more militaristic.

Assassination. Finally, the trigger for WWI was the assassination of Archduke Franz Ferdinand. The Slavic people from the areas of Bosnia and Herzegovina no longer wanted to belong to Austria-Hungary, because they believed that Slavic people should be able to unite together as one nation. The resulting ethnic revolt was the primary trigger for WWI.

Archduke Franz Ferdinand was assassinated by Gavrilo Princip, a member of a Serbian Nationalist group called the "Black Hand". This happened on 28 June 1914 at Sarajevo in Bosnia. The Archduke was next in line to the throne of Austria so this came as a huge shock and an attack on Austrian sovereignty. Vienna wanted retaliation. They insisted on harsh demands which the Serbians refused and Austria declared War on Serbia on 28 July 1914. Germany agreed to supply Austria with men and weapons and so Russia declared War on Germany, followed by Germany declaring War on Russia. On 3 August Germany declared War on Frame. The next day Britain declared War on Germany. On 6 August Austria declared War on Russia and by the end of August Japan was also at war with Austria and Germany. It was only in 2017 that the US declared War on Germany.

As you can see, the beginning of World War I, which arose from a culture of nationalism, imperialism and militarism started Iike a child's game of dominoes, where one falls and starts a chain reaction that topples them all. In a matter of two months, a huge part of the world was at war. This was exacerbated by colonization, which meant that subjects of the countries at war from all over the world, Australia, New Zealand, Africa, India, Canada, and other parts of Asia, were drawn into the struggle.

Chapter Four
The Lead Up to the Battle of the Somme and the mistakes made by Military Leadership

The British and French military leaders committed to the Battle at the Somme in 1915 during the Chantilly Conference. It was meant to relieve the pressure on the French by the aggressive German attack. A strategy was developed for battles by the Russian, French, British, and Italian armies, with the Somme being a Franco-British effort. The main forces were intended to be French with the British supporting them on the northern flank. Unfortunately for the British forces, the Battle of Verdun, which began on 21 February took away most of the French troops intended for the Somme, and the British forces were, in fact, urgently required to deflect German troops from the ferocious attack at Verdun. The supporting attack by Britain became the principal attack—one by a particularly inexperienced group of soldiers or officers, being largely Herbert Kitchener's army that was a new volunteer force. These were bolstered by the remaining pre-war army and some of the territorial forces.

On Day 1 of the Somme, the bloodiest in British military history, the Germans suffered a severe defeat at the hands of the French Sixth Army. The British, however, attacked where the German defenses were strongest between Albert-Bapaume Road and Gommecourt.

By the end of the battle 141 days later, the British and French troops had gained only 6 miles of territory and their principal objectives were not achieved, because they failed to force the Germans' retreat from Peronne and Bapaume. The Germans finally retreated behind the Hindenburg line only in March the following year.

The failure of the Battle of the Somme to reach its military objectives was because of the extremely compact battlefield combined with very high bombardment by modern weaponry and some extremely bad decisions made by British military leadership.

The concentration of the battlefield and the German doctrine that they would never surrender even a yard of their territory, made for extremely fierce fighting, especially as the British and French leadership were not prepared to give up the attack.

The horrific casualties and deaths experienced on both sides of more than a million men indicate the frightening amount of armaments unleashed into a very small space. The entire front was only 18 miles along the River Somme.

The Battle was never expected to be harsh. General Sir Douglas Haig had ordered a week-long bombardment of more than a million shells before the battle and obviously believed that the German trenches had taken sufficient punishment and were ripe for plundering, but in fact, it was discovered afterward that half the shells did not detonate, that the German trenches were largely undamaged and their barbed wire fortifications remained intact.

The officers assured the soldiers that, as a result of this heavy bombardment, there would be very few Germans left to fight. The Germans, however, were well prepared. They had used the chalk downs to good effect and created a maze of deep trenches with excellent supply fortifications in the rear and properly installed buried communication lines.

When the British and French forces went "over the top" at 7.30 on the first day of the battle, they were expecting minimal resistance, but they were destroyed by the counterattack. They were weighed down by heavy gear, like shovels, which they planned to use to shore up the enemy trenches which they expected to be damaged and unusable. There were no anticipated gaps in the barbed wire, but as they clustered round to find them, they were easy targets for German fire. A later report from the Germans claimed that they "didn't even have to aim." The soldiers fell in their thousands.

What is rather shocking is that General Haig, even after the overwhelming casualties on the first day and the obvious realization that they had misjudged the effects of the bombardment, ordered the attack to continue. The weaponry was excessive with tons of artillery shells, machine guns, chemical weapons, flamethrowers, and even tanks.

Basically, the soldiers on both sides were just fodder in a battle of attrition, and it became obvious early that any territory gains on the Western Front were going to be hard won.

This terrible death toll which continued day after day, despite the commander's eventually reducing the scale of the personnel attack to try to save lives, is the reason why the Battle of the Somme is highly criticized, even today, as an act of madness. But was it? History has differing opinions, which we will examine later.

The initial attack on 1 July 1916 was launched by 120 000 Allied troops from England and the colonies like South Africa, Australia, India, New Zealand, Canada, and Newfoundland. Of those 120 000 soldiers, 20 000 were killed on the first day. Most of them were killed in the first hour, and 37 000 soldiers were wounded. A man was killed every 4.4 seconds. The tally at the end of the day showed that 37 pairs of British brothers were killed on that first day. One can just imagine the heartbreak for the families at home. This was the single bloodiest day in the history of British battles.

The trigger for WWI was the assassination of Archduke Franz Ferdinand. The Slavic people from the areas of Bosnia and Herzegovina no longer wanted to belong to Austria-Hungary, because they believed that Slavic people should be able to unite together as one nation. The resulting ethnic revolt was the primary trigger for WWI.

Chapter Five

The Somme - What it was like on the Battlefield. Some eyewitness accounts.

Section 1: The First Day Of The Somme

"There wasn't one of us in our battalion that ever got to the German lines ....it was impossible." — Donald Murray

Private Donald Murray, born in 1893, was one of the voices on the podcast series, *The Voices of the Somme*. He explained that they were aware from early in May that they were training for something really big. They had laid out the entire battlefield, 10 km back from the line with all the German lines flagged out. Then, they started to bring heavy artillery to the front of the line.

Other soldiers, too, commented on the huge numbers of heavy weaponry and train loads of shells that kept arriving. They were told that there would not be a German soldier for miles after the heavy bombardment and that they would easily take the German trenches.

Section 2: The Bombardment

The intensive week of the bombardment was described by Artillery Officer Maurice Laws. He described the intensive bombardment from dawn to dusk every day. A fatigue party brought food and water at dusk every day, but otherwise, the assault was ongoing. As the observation officer for the battery, he described the noise and the fatigue they all experienced. The Royal Artillery fired more than 1.6 million shells. The noise was described as "a dance of hell" by Harry Wheeler, a British Signaller who swore that 60 years later, he could still hear the artillery noise.

A German soldier, Stephen Westmann described the bombardment as "incessant," saying that they were always digging out their comrades, some of whom were suffocated and smashed to pieces. They had no food and soldiers kept getting hysterical trying to escape the bombardment. Even the rats tried to escape the terrible onslaught.

Nonetheless, we know from history that the damage to the German lines was not severe enough to make the English attack easy but that the casualties on all sides were terrible.

Section 3: Private Maurice Symes

On 1 July, the first day of the battle, 40 000 men were wounded. Private Maurice Symes was one of them. He explained how they stepped over the top trenches, and he saw men falling all around him. Then he got shot and described how it "kicked me in the stomach; a funny sort of feeling but I knew I couldn't go any further...I had a bullet straight through, then I got into a shell hole for a bit of shelter and got another shrapnel wound there."

Another soldier explained the feeling of abject fear of not knowing what to do, whether to get up and go or stop and wait. He described it as immobilizing. This was exacerbated by the absence of direct orders because of high officer casualties. The soldiers were being mowed down and no one told them how to continue.

One soldier described the scene at the German lines, with soldiers lying dead or screaming or hanging on barbed wire with their bowels hanging out. It was a scene out of hell. He could find no other living people, so he crept back to the trenches and gradually other survivors joined him. The officers were surprised to see him. They did not think anyone had survived.

Most eyewitness accounts describe this battle as a scene of such horror, such chaos, and such disorder that it felt practically surreal, particularly as the survivors dwindled daily.

Chapter Six

The Second Battle of the Somme

Section 1: 21 March to 4 April 1918

Many people don't realize that a second Battle of the Somme took place in 1918. It was significant mainly because of the arrival of American troops, which finally saw off the exhausted German forces and bolstered the numbers and morale of the British and French forces.

On March 21, 1918, the Germans began an important attack against the Allied forces in the Somme River area of France. This started with more than five hours of blitzing from more than 9,000 pieces of guns and other artillery. The British Fifth Army, which was largely unprepared, was quickly overwhelmed and forced into a rather ignominious retreat. The line was all but broken. The German commander, General Erich Ludendorff, had thought that it was important for Germany to utilize the troops which had been freed from the Eastern Front after the final collapse of Russia to secure a victory on the Western Front before the American soldiers came to reinforce Allies who were, as the Germans were, exhausted by years of war. For the next week, the Germans made a push toward Paris. They shelled the city from an impressive distance of more than 80 miles with a long-range gun. The German name for it was the "Kaiser Wilhelm Geschütz," but the Parisians named it, the "Big Bertha," and had a hearty respect for it.

Section 2: The Outcome

The German troops were undersupplied and exhausted from years of war and quickly ran out of steam. The Allies retaliated with force and the Germans were prevented from attacking and besieging Paris by the French artillery, which knocked the German guns out.

On 2 April, General John Pershing of the US forces sent US troops into the French trenches to help them. This was interestingly the first major showing by US troops during WWI, and the couple of thousand American soldiers, fresh to war, brought new hope and stamina to the exhausted French and British troops. No wonder the Germans could not hold their positions. It's hard to imagine how little stomach for fighting the troops on both sides must have had after 4 years of war.

Section 3: The end of German dominance?

After the battle of the Somme, which ended on 4 April, the Americans had made some important gains. They advanced almost 40 miles, captured 70 000 prisoners, and inflicted nearly 200 000 casualties. The Germans also suffered heavy casualties, and as they did not have the reprieve of the arrival of American soldiers, they were finally repelled.

By the time of the second battle of the Somme, Germany, generally, was on the back foot. With the US entering the war, there was a sudden abundance of fresh fighting men and virtually unlimited access to new supplies, which the Germans did not have despite the war-weary soldiers coming from the Eastern front.

Although the second Somme proved to be one of the biggest territorial gains of WWI, it exhausted German supplies and stamina and could not be sustained.

Are You Enjoying Reading?

As an independent publisher

with a tiny marketing budget

we rely on readers, like you.

If you're receiving help from this book,

would you please take a moment to write a brief review?

We really appreciate it.

Are You Enjoying Reading?

Chapter Seven

Was the Somme a defeat?

Section 1: A pointless battle of Attrition

"Human flesh is powerless to withstand that amount of destruction." —
Private Spencer Jones

The Battle of the Somme seems like the height of pointlessness with nearly a million casualties in just over four months. The battle seems both ill-planned, ill-judged and extremely wasteful as the battle plan didn't even consider looking at the human catastrophe, the pain, the loss to families, the cost of hospitalization and rehabilitation from often very severe injuries, and the effects on the future lives of survivors whether injured or not.

Was the Somme a defeat? Certainly, the British forces did not achieve their goals, but they did reduce the effects of the attack in Verdun. The battle was a stalemate on both sides as only 6 miles of French territory was retaken. And the loss of life for that achievement was so absurd that it could have been called a resounding defeat. It comes down to semantics in the end whether those 6 miles really amounted to anything in the grander context of WWI. History has not decided whether the Battle of the Somme was a defeat or not.

Section 2: Did the Somme cause tactical Changes?

The Somme could be called a training ground for war mistakes to be made and the changes in tactics to happen so that the future of the war could be less wasteful and bloody and certainly, that future battles and wars could be fought differently. As history taught us time and again, we never know how one decision can impact the future. Battles like the Somme might have led directly to strategic decisions being made. For example, the exorbitant cost entailed by land battles and trench warfare, led the Germans to shift their resources and strategies towards submarine attacks, which affected the United States with the sinking of the Lusitania and led to the Americans entering the war when they perceived a threat to their sovereign territory, and this, of course, gave the Allies the advantage leading to their final victory. If the Americans had not entered the war, then one wonders what the outcome would have been. Russia had effectively been defeated and forced to sue for peace, and the war-weary allies were ill-equipped to continue the fight on the Western front. Did the disastrous Battle of the Somme facilitate this? One certainly wonders.

Section 3: A Stepping Stone?

Although the Battle of the Somme was a ghastly and wasteful human experience, some modern historians classify it as an important "stepping stone" to victory in 1918. We will be examining this in more detail in Point 9. It's difficult to assess what might have happened if battles like the Somme had not forced the military leadership to rethink their warfare strategies, because hindsight is an exact science, and we have no way of really knowing what might have happened, but taken at face value, the Battle of the Somme was so wasteful and so terrible that its effects could not be ignored in future strategies.

The Trenches of Death- One soldier described the scene at the German

lines with soldiers lying dead or screaming or hanging on barbed wire

with their bowels hanging out. It was a scene out of hell. He could find no

other living people, so he crept back to the trenches and gradually other survivors joined him. The officers were surprised to see him. They did not think anyone had survived.

On 2 April, General John Pershing of the US forces sent US troops into the French trenches to help them. This was interestingly the first major showing by US troops during WWI, and the couple of thousand American soldiers, fresh to war, brought new hope and stamina to the exhausted French and British troops. No wonder the Germans could not hold their positions. It's hard to imagine how little stomach for fighting the troops on both sides must have had after 4 years of war.

Chapter Eight
The Lessons from the Somme

One cannot emphasize enough the tragedy of the Battle of the Somme to both sides. Neither should one neglect to acknowledge the lessons that were learned from the battle.

Section 1: The Inexperienced soldiers of the Somme

The Battle of Somme went down in history as one of the most infamous battles of WWI. As we have discussed, the first day of this terrible battle is infamous for the British army as the bloodiest day in its whole history. This is partly because of the inexperienced men and officers who fought the battle. Many of the soldiers were part of the volunteer corps who after about a year of training, started to see active service in early 1916, mainly on the Western Front. Because of this, the Battle of the Somme, which was the largest battle yet launched by the British Army, was the first one to be fought by a citizen army which was constituted of civilian volunteers rather than by experienced professional soldiers. This unfortunately meant that without battlefield experience, they were very vulnerable.

Section 2: The Miners of Somme

This battle was not just fought in no-man's land. Under the ground, British and German engineers fought a terrible silent war as they tunneled and counter-tunneled and engaged in hand-to-hand fighting and explosives.

Archeologists discovered a host of tunnels and caves in the chalk downs of the Somme. These had been unopened for over 100 years and had signatures and poetry graffitied on the walls from soldiers of the Cumbrian regiment who were fighting an underground war.

These tunnelers attacked the same day as the land attack began. They worked as backup and labor for the Royal Engineers, carrying out rubble and engaging in hand-to-hand combat with the Germans.

Section 3: Battle Hardened

After almost 5 months of fighting, the inexperienced volunteer soldiers had become battle-hardened. This was also true of the officers who had to learn to fight a war on this scale. They made improvements to their battle tactics and the introduction of new weapons, including tanks all were part of their learning strategy. The tanks were largely hopeless, but they paved the way for better quality ones. The initial descriptions of the first days of the battle, which showed terrified men wandering aimlessly around, changed as the commanders and soldiers started to think of ways to minimize casualties and maximize their effectiveness. While the Allied forces paid extremely highly in casualties, so did the Germans who began to see the British soldiers as formidable opponents.

Nonetheless, many British citizens to this day believe that the British Army paid unacceptably high school fees for the lessons learned by the end of the Battle of the Somme. Whether they are right or not, very few British families were unaffected by WWI, and they are within their rights to criticize what was a very badly planned and executed battle, whatever the long-term outcome.

Chapter Nine
Some men behind the Somme

Wars are about men managing men and men fighting for their country and their beliefs. The human element is very important and should never be denied. In this section, we'll look at the brains or lack thereof behind the Battle and also at one hero, who epitomized the courage of the British Tommy.

Section 1: The heroes - Billy McFadzean

The story of Billy McFadzean was a tragic one. He gave his life for his comrades before the actual fighting even started. A 20-year-old rifleman, 6 foot tall, Billy was a strapping rugby player who came to the trenches as a bomber.

Billy was given the job of carrying buckets of hand grenades to the top of the trenches so they were available for the soldiers who were going over the top. At this stage, a box of bombs, which was open for attack slipped and Billy became aware that two hand grenades had lost their pins.

He threw himself on the box and absorbed the impact. He died instantly but as a result of his courage, only one other man was injured. He was posthumously awarded the Victoria Cross.

Billy had said in a letter to his parents, "I hope to play the game and if I don't add much luster to it, I certainly will not tarnish it." And he certainly didn't. He died a hero but he also received rather dubious fame for being the first death of the Somme. Only hours later he was joined by thousands of his comrades.

Section 2: Sir Douglas Haig

Field Marshal Sir Douglas Haig was an experienced soldier who had seen action in India, Sudan, and the Boer War. Nonetheless, he never really lived down his role in the Somme and was popularly known as "the butcher." He failed to make the anticipated breakthrough in the Somme and Verdun. He also refused to back down and give up when the battles were going their way at the Somme. He was accused by history of allowing battles of attrition to continue long after strategic advantage had been lost. Whether or not this is true is a question for historians. Haig certainly denied it himself.

Section 3: Sir Henry Rawlinson

A phrase arose during WWI, which was commonly applied to Haig and to Sir Henry Rawlinson who commanded the actual troops. Rawlinson devised or implemented the policy where men were to walk in orderly rows following behind their commanding officers. On the first day of the Battle of the Somme, the Germans were bemused to see British troops armed with revolvers or batons walking towards their trenches. The bemusement did not last long, and they opened fire on the easy targets creating the famous first-day slaughter for which the Somme became known.

During WWI and afterward, Haig and Rawlinson were popularly known as the "donkeys," who while being both distant and incompetent, sent the "lions" (the British Infantry) to their deaths. The Somme did nothing to dispel this notion.

Chapter Ten
Was the Somme worth it?

Section 1: Questions from History

History has asked the question of whether or not the devastating loss of life at the Battle of Somme and similar battles was worth it. While popular opinion says no, and trench warfare was abandoned after WWI, historians have differed. We'll have a look at two differing opinions from two Canadian historians who saw the terrible loss of life of their own countrymen.

Section 2: Jonathan Vance says No

Jonathan Vance is a Professor of History at Western University Ontario and the author of many books about wars. These include *Death So Noble: Memory, Meaning and the First World War* and *Maple Leaf Empire*.

Vance reiterates that Field Marshal Sir Douglas Haig, at the Chantilly Conference in November 1916, definitely thought the war effort at the Somme was not in vain. Haig concluded in his report that the Somme had achieved its objectives. Verdun had been relieved. The Allies had held the German forces on the Western Front, and the military strength of the Germans had been "very considerably worn down."

However, Vance is particularly critical of those words of Haig's. He agrees that battles of attrition were inevitable in WWI, where the powers fighting were too strong to be beaten by a decisive blow, but he argues that the Somme was not a "bite and hold" defensive. It was planned as a decisive stroke. It was meant to be a strong definitive attack that would destroy the German hold in that area. It became a Battle of Attrition because Haig failed to make it definitive with a badly planned and executed bombardment at the beginning. To pat himself on the back for achieving the goal of weakening the German army is to fail to look at the effects on the British army. It took another two long years for the German army to show significant weakness.

Military leadership was themselves muddled by the brief of the Somme. Some thought it was to gain ground. Others thought it was to offer a crippling blow. This muddled planning and general confusion were a feature of the Somme.

Section 3: Andrew Iarocci says Yes

Andrew Iarocci is Assistant Professor in the History Department at Western University and wrote *Shoestring Soldiers: The First Canadian Division, 1914-15.*

Iarocci agrees that the defense was full of misunderstandings and errors which led to unnecessary loss of human life for a very little gain of ground, but his argument is that "if the First World War was worth fighting, then the Battle of the Somme was worth the cost." He believed that the battle contributed to the final success of the war. The Germans took the bait to hold onto every inch of soil and lost as many men and gained even less. These cost strategies eventually caused the Germans to change some of their policies, which, as previously discussed, had the effect of drawing America into the war.

The mistakes from the Somme also taught the British commanders more effective and less bloody battle strategies which helped them to win further battles and, ultimately, the war.

Field Marshal Sir Douglas Haig was an experienced soldier who had seen action in India, Sudan, and the Boer War. Nonetheless, he never really lived down his role in the Somme and was popularly known as "the butcher." He failed to make the anticipated breakthrough in the Somme and Verdun. He also refused to back down and give up when the battles were going the way of the Somme. He was accused by history of allowing battles of attrition to continue long after strategic advantage had been lost.

Whether or not this is true is a question for historians. Haig certainly denied it himself.

Sir Henry Rawlinson - During WWI and afterward, Haig and Rawlinson were popularly known as the "donkeys," who while being both distant and incompetent, sent the "lions" (the British Infantry) to their deaths. The Somme did nothing to dispel this notion.

Chapter Eleven
The Celebration of the Somme

The story of the Somme as one of the battles of WWI has been represented in so many ways. Thousands of articles, academic papers, and journals have been written about it. It's been represented in poetry, in books, and fictional and factual literature.

The horrifying statistics of the Somme—the casualties were 420 000 British, 200 000 French, and 500 000 German soldiers—were so dramatic that they attracted the attention of writers and filmmakers.

One of the most interesting and dramatic representations of the Battle was actual footage released in the silent movie entitled *The Battle of the Somme*. The British war office allowed the filming of the actual battle because they believed they were going to win it, and they thought it would motivate and inspire people.

Filmmakers Geoffrey Malins and John McDowell used actual Somme scenes and added them to staged battle scenes. Some scenes, like the tossing of bodies into communal graves shocked and dismayed the watching public, many of whom actually hoped to catch a glimpse of a husband, son, or brother in the actual footage. Twenty million people saw the film within a few months, and it remains one of the most watched films in British history. This is particularly relevant in a time when there were only 43 million Britons.

One horrifying scene, believed to be taken on the first day of the battle, although actually staged, shows a Tommy soldier dying 30 minutes after he arrived in the trenches. The movie was meant to be an encouraging and motivational one that would show Britain that their soldiers were being well cared for and that the war was being won by the Allies, but it actually created a lot of anxiety, fear, and a realization of the actual horrors of war. It escaped censorship because it was actually a propaganda movie, but surprisingly, it represented the horrors of war very effectively. The iconic moment in the film when the soldiers go over the top was actually staged, but it gave a real sense that war was horrific, terrifying, and not in any way glorious. This made the production a very authentic and effective one. Although it was a propagandistic one, the movie managed to avoid cliches about the Germans being villains and the Allies being honorable and decent. This is what most of Britain already believed, so they were not influenced by the objectivity of the film.

The film did hide the extent of the casualties on the first day and showed the British soldiers being more cheerful and optimistic than their German counterparts, but other than this, it was a genuinely realistic representation of the horrors of the Somme.

Memorials to the Battle of the Somme and other battles are widely spread across France and in the UK and, in fact, in every colony. The Thiepval Memorial is a famous Somme memorial dedicated to the 72 337 British and South African soldiers who lost their lives in the two battles of the Somme and have no known grave. It is a very poignant memorial and one which is popular with tourists.

The Thiepval Memorial is a famous Somme memorial that is dedicated to the 72 337 British and South African soldiers who lost their lives in the two battles of the Somme and have no known grave. It is a very poignant memorial and one which is popular with tourists.

Chapter Twelve
Conclusion

The Battle of the Somme (July 1–Nov 18 1916), was an Allied battle in World War I. The British and French troops initiated a frontal assault against the entrenched German battalions on the north side of the Somme River. An artillery bombardment that took a week and was meant to cripple the Germans was followed by an infantry attack by the British forces on the German positions which were still impenetrable. There were almost 60 000 British casualties (including 20 000 fatalities) on the first day of the battle which slowly worsened into a full-scale battle of attrition, impeded by torrential downpours in October that rendered the muddy battleground impassable. By the time the battle was discontinued, the Allies had progressed only 6 miles. The enormous casualties included 650 000 Germans, 420 000 British, and 195 000 French. The Battle of the Somme became an analogy for the fruitless and indiscriminate massacre created by war.

In the sections that we have examined, it's increasingly clear that at the very best, historians believe the Battle of the Somme was necessary because it taught valuable lessons for future battles and that it might have caused the Germans to give up on trench warfare and concentrate on the submarine warfare that brought the US into the war. At the very worst and reflecting popular opinion, it was seen as an unwarranted bloodbath and a huge failure.

The casualties of any war are not only physical; the men who came back from the Battle of the Somme and from other wars were emotionally scarred. Psychologists believe that a whole generation of emotionally dysfunctional men and families arose because of their reactions to the horrors of witnessing and being part of such terrible events. The philosophy of the stiff upper lip meant that men seldom spoke of their experiences and without trauma counseling, situations of wife and child abuse, anger management problems and depression were part of the package.

But regardless of this, no true Briton to this day would have wanted their men not to have gone to war and fought for the values they believed in which is why Remembrance Day and other celebrations of war are so loved even more than 100 years later.

Here are poignant words from Taps which buglers played every night as the soldiers went to rest and at the funeral or memorial of every soldier.

Day is done, Gone the sun,

From the lake, From the hill,

From the sky.

All is well, Safely rest,

God is nigh.

Thanks and praise, For our days,

Neath the sun, Neath the stars,

Neath the sky,

As we go, This we know,

God is nigh.

Fades the light; And afar

Goeth day, And the stars

Shineth bright,

Fare thee well; Day has gone,

Night is on.

Go to sleep, Peaceful sleep,

May the Soldier or Sailor,

God keep.

On the land or the deep,

Safe in sleep.

Love, good night, Must thou go,

When the day, And the night

Need thee so?

All is well. Speedeth all

To their rest.

Chapter Thirteen

Discussion Question

Was the Battle of the Somme worth it? Examine the evidence in the text and decide whether you agree with the value of the battle or not. Justify your answer.

Discussion Question

The Battle of the Somme was early in World War I. What lessons did commanders learn from the mistakes made in the battle? How did this influence the outcome of the war?

Discussion Question

What did you learn about the average British Tommy from the texts you have just read? Do you feel sympathy for the German forces too? What motivated your opinion?

Discussion Question

Do you enjoy the examples of war poetry from this period? Do you find them relevant to the experience of war? Do you agree with the sentiments expressed?

Discussion Question

What is your opinion of trench warfare after reading about the battle of the Somme? Is it effective? Justify your response.

Discussion Question

Did you think Sir Douglas Haig was a "butcher"? Describe the personality of the man from what you have read. Was he typical of the commanders of the time?

Discussion Question

Imagine that you were part of the trench warfare at the Battle of the Somme. How would it make you feel? Why do you think the soldiers were so brave?

Discussion Question

Explain why the silent movie *The Battle of the Somme* was so popular. Do you think that watching battle scenes would make people resistant to war or not? Explain this in conjunction with the notes on Nationalism and Patriotism.

Chapter Fourteen

Quiz Question

1. **True/False:** The Battle of the Somme was held in France. The objective was to relieve pressure on Verdun. It was an Allied push.

2. **True/False:** The Battle of Somme was a definitive victory for the Allies. It put the Germans under severe pressure. It can be called one of the success stories of the war.

3. **True/False:** The first day of the Battle of the Somme was the bloodiest in British military history. More men died than on any other day. It was carnage.

4. **True/False:** The Germans were unaffected by the Battle of the Somme. Their losses were minimal. They were safe in their tunnels.

5. **True/ False:** The Americans came into the war because the Germans got disgruntled with trench warfare. They started a submarine war. They sank an American passenger ship.

6. **True/False:** The commanders at the Battle of the Somme let the men run and zigzag and dive for cover. They allowed a defensive attack. They were protective of the safety of the soldiers.

7. **True/False:** One of the heroes of the Somme was killed before the war even began. He threw himself into a box of hand grenades. That killed him but saved his colleagues.

8. **True/ False:** The movie *The Battle of the Somme* sold 2 million tickets. It was a box office hit. Britons love war movies.

Quiz Answer

1. True

2. False: It was a very minimal success with only 6 miles of land gained after 141 days of battle.

3. True

4. False: They had casualties of 500,000.

5. True

6. False: They made them walk slowly in straight lines to their doom.

7. True

8. False: It had 20 million watchers.

Bibliography

- The Battle of the Somme. Wikipedia Commons.

  https://upload.wikimedia.org/wikipedia/commons/thumb/a/ac/

  The_Battle_of_the_Somme%2C_July-

  november_1916_Q3970.jpg/608px-

  The_Battle_of_the_Somme%2C_July-november_1916_Q3970.jpg

- Arch Duke Ferdinand. Wikipedia.

  https://en.wikipedia.org/wiki/Archduke_Franz_Ferdinand_of_Aust

  ria#/media/File:Ferdinand_Schmutzer_-

  _Franz_Ferdinand_von_%C3%96sterreich-Este,_um_1914.jpg

- The Trenches of Death. Getty Images.

  https://www.gettyimages.com/detail/news-photo/blotted-out-

  while-the-terrific-battle-swept-on-these-dead-news-

  photo/515465632?adppopup=true Bettmann.

- Battle of the Somme Soldiers. Wikimedia Commons.

  https://commons.wikimedia.org/wiki/File:First_day_of_the_Battle_

  of_the_Somme_%2836122542172%29.png

- Sir Douglas Haig. SNL. https://snl.no/Douglas_Haig

- Sir Henry Rawlinson. Wikimedia Commons. https://en.wikipedia.org/wiki/Henry_Rawlinson,_1st_Baron_Rawlinson

- The Thiepval Memorial. Wikimedia. https://commons.wikimedia.org/wiki/File:Thiepval_Memorial_to_the_missing.jpg

Bonus Downloads

*Get Free Books with **Any Purchase** History Shorts*

Every purchase comes with a FREE download!